Resurrection of the Poet

by

ELLIE
ROWAN

Village Books Publishing

Bellingham, Washington

Hardcover ISBN: 9780578974422

Library of Congress Control Number: 2021917044

First hardcover edition November 2021.

Book design © by Amanda Costello of Amanda Costello Design, LLC
Cover art © by Ellie Rowan
Edited by Ellie Rowan

Printed in The United States of America by Village Books.

Village Books
1200 11th Street
Bellingham, WA 98225

Resurrection of the Poet

Dedication

They happen all around us – these moments of unforeseen certainty; certainty of a piece inside and what we make of it; what we become *for* it.

At the beginning of this year, I had a conversation with someone about such matters.

"So what black swan events would you prepare for?"

Now jumping to the branch of mathematics known as chaos theory, these poems held up a mirror and became one of many ways that I began to see myself, after the butterfly effect that took form in hearing that question and my response, came to life.

May you find matter in these words from which to effect and for how you imagine them to be, they are yours.

———————

We Became

Underneath; above all:
to be young yet,
new again.
Sung yet again,
always to be distinct
with every reason and so,
free of all.
May pain and beauty be seen,
we may find reasons change –
only to observe that we could.
The stories
of adaptation's alternative
came to light before,
so, for such we became.
In a world that shows colors we may hope to place,
we may only begin to see them
when we unsee ourselves,
to meet ourselves.
All in care,
free to care.

Here Still

Everywhere yet here,
is where we wanted to be.
Everywhere we went then –
so we changed where we went,
because then we wanted to be here.

How So

There
it was with us again
at that time,
feeling feelings and feeling that they were
to be treasured –
held close,
protected,
to be set free.

How that feels.

To yet again do so,
to yet again believe,
to yet again see
that in time –
such is beautiful,
always bright,
always fiery,
always loud with life.

When life is loud with you.

How that feels.

Patience Without Weight

These words were made to become alive,
these words were made to adapt;
to heal.
Made to pull us through; guide us through.
These words are only our own, all our own.
They gave us peace,
patience,
understanding,
security in existence –
Only for our choice further past.
These words were our path to life;
life gave to us these words.

To Meet Again

We were in the month of June,
as she was
when seen back in February.
Yet earlier even,
was wondered if
we could be like that woman again –
that woman on the rock watching over the bay.
She saw that it had always been.
Back then, she had always seen.
So to have seen her then,
at peace to have seen her again,
so hoped to meet her again.
We wished for her, that wherever she went next –
whether that be to October, earlier,
or somewhere else –
that she may remain intact with June
and forever confident
in February;
earlier even.

So She Will

After all,
what unseen was the same,
what unheard was unchanged.
Inevitably they arrived
to do more;
to be more.
What lies still:
something to be seen by *her*,
though *her* they have already seen.
Forever to be speaking so she can,
forever to be faster so she can.
Learning from and for her,
for one and another,
for all, as there is one in the same.
For after all,
they are young yet new –
what could they think to be possible
if possibility so let them?
Let's ask her.

Still

Fiery and bright,
in time
a deficit in animation
so caught us.
For we were rather fixed to be,
and we were rather fast.
Could absence become even more so,
we were greater still –
a crossing to see just once more
our infinite vitality.

To Reach

These moments
of prostration –
we could see what more.
And time began,
so we saw more.
We were untouchable,
to forever reach higher.

We have felt many smiles, loud and clear –
and the laughter touched our lives from far away.

A life everchanging,
ours as such:
because we found unmatched fun here,
than in anything once more.

In Progression

There forward,
we were forever masters in our change:
forever choosing how to process;
progress our change.
We were forever granting such responses;
us.
Forever here forever more,
to note our intention always –
we became champions of this life,
that which is ours.
That,
is what we share between us.

To yet again choose,
because it is there that we were found to be
realized,
actualized,
let go of.

Thus, we choose yet again.

The Lights

We had a dream
of the city,
and in turn,
of us it dreamt –
so here, we went.
There, we are.

Intact

We take ourselves everywhere:
we can start anywhere.

We go there:
a trip around the yard,
       barred still we are.
A trip around the street,
       by our feet we were unfelt.
A trip around the neighborhood,
       the flood we so began.
So a trip around the city –
       our weathered storm polished yet.
A trip around the state-
       could we have been there –
yet we answer with "Hello next country!"
       And next country responds –
so we go to the next country,
       and the next,
       and we meet always such
in new friendships,
       books,
       roads,
       bike trails,
       dance moves,
       stories,
       beaches –
and we are born again:
forever ourselves,
forever intact:
to be lost,
to be changed,
to be ourselves forever stronger; forever more.

Beautiful Night

Mountains engulfing,
a firm hug left content
to look up:
sky wonderous,
fiery and from day's temperature –
then soft, blue, green and resting,
water falling and this one star,
only as near as it twinkles.
Thoughts came still,
and that was just fine.
Presence was steadied,
hands were held;
we were pulled to be
only and exactly where we were –
gently, of course.

Home

It may be wherever,
whoever
or whenever –
that our feelings
are freed to be only of the beholder,
and ours more.
It may be simple –
to here we could return.
Unbound we are,
unfettered to need not consider
who that is.
To desire our association,
and from such we fly more.
To be reminded in first
our comfort in self,
could only we ever become
so much past.
Our credence to step outside
transformed:
we flew with conviction
in our hopes to share
and be given a share of this.

Eyes Into Gold

Only like that,
out of nowhere
and because of everywhere –
there we saw it again.
Right as it was felt so,
right as it stood to be so.
As could always be there,
she was always found,
so yet again someone else was
seen.

Sent Through the Heart

How ludicrous,
to have been poised
to be commented –
to have been tried in decided
such experiences,
feelings and thoughts
when so removed from
our heart they endured.
How untouchable we became,
so that all we may touch,
and may we too,
be touched.

Commemoration

A fight of the minds,
from an ascendancy of a mind
to behold.
For the moves to be written across
walls only theirs,
from our words we were lifted
to release their speech
so as to lift us more.
In liberation:
inaction,
inertia,
desperation
may give light
to sallow hearts once more:
only then could they too
ignite
for all,
and for all
to fortify.
For we were guided through
in stepping out of their dualism,
so as to celebrate our integration
of so much more than
two.

What Was Yours

Could you do so much
though too to
arrogate so much in a way;
of one way
to feel,
to express,
so as to suffer remembrance
of what was yours
to begin with?

Unmissable

In our world to be ours,
creation may ours become.
Lives belonging to us,
though only ours yet we become alive.
Experiences just the same,
thoughts all the same –
feelings one in the same.
To hold ours is for us that which we safeguard:
such same experience,
thoughts
and feelings.
May we meet inclinations unmissable,
we may give way
to safeguard such over that which
we already did; being
experiences,
thoughts
and feelings.

We could only be curious,
we could yet try,
we may only want
to have them.

This Rosebud

Irrefutable it may be –
and perhaps so yet to be seen,
to have regard for the people;
people that have caught us
before reason
to be seen.
How when this rose
to our recognition,
we understood that to be too,
could be relieved of reason unheard.

Our Tune

These moments
are for dancing to our step,
as are those for singing devotedly.
Make space we might
for the moments of soft smiles and gentle hums.
For we may cry and scream as we go,
as we can flow again
may we be engulfed again yet.
While in moments of then
we thought to be in place,
we then moved forth from beyond.
As on occasion our steps led us to be overcome so,
it is our occasion for which to always raise.
For these songs,
as multifaceted as they may be –
may give way to the perspective
of their counterparts.
We only thought this to be so,
and so counterparts we became.

We are always at the dancing part again,
yet again.

Howdy Again

Thought about it,
in everything done and undone –

for the shimmer seen,
was to be found everywhere; every place
looked after.

Gorgeous – that we always could, though unheard of yet to be.

To meet again,
and again
there we went:

always,

us.

We May Be

This may only have been for us:
it could have been,
then once again,
as it may be,
infinitely,
if we want.
For now,
if we so choose.
For later,
if it be so.

To have seen
all of one, multiplied how many else:
all of one.

We wanted even more,
and so realized,
we could be attained
so as to see even more.

We picked up this pen yet again,
for to have illustrated what was,
we may have illustrated
for what could be
more:
it may be the most that could be.

Mirage

In originating words
of the existence
for entities so outside,
we may too
shed only an illusion.
May we
hear them to be
see them to be
observe them to be
how they present to be.
Though even as we are
freestanding,
how could we hear
our own words to be only such,
may we disarm
and inevitably so
be led to our words
again
not just once more.

Willed

We so dreamt
of a moment:
one hand in hand with many,
simple will and oblivious to thought;
where to say "yes"
with everything,
and so be it such word only washed over.
What on earth could that be,
what on earth that could become:
unreal,
for it may be
for some place else.
The step then –
how to exist with impatience
for life;
could be here waiting for you,
may be waiting with you –
to so choose it
to be.

These Other Things

Shivering, here wishing while wondering
could the sun be bigger and brighter –
when a bird descended
for a lap or two around the tree.
Plant matter floated past,
as did these reminders
in time and time inform:
that when it was cold it was never just cold,
it was these other things too.
And these other things
could still the shivers and smile so warm,
when we may not have done it alone.

Shattered Together

Those ones
were yet it all,
all that embodies,
all they could become:
gave them sight, too.
Divided
so as to piece together
on a night shining in essence,
rose the golden sun again
to day,
glistening because they were forever bonded.

Omega

May these thoughts
move faster than their speech,
we could have distressed,
losing one moment to the next.
Anchored still,
we may have met each moment
faster than before
here for the next.
As tomorrow is unchanged,
so opposite we are constantly.
As right now is unchanged,
only we may commence.

Yours to Keep

Grasping,
refashioning,
receiving:
all for beyond.

We transformed before our end:
incomprehensible;
nonexistent.
For the way it may have felt
is for how we may feel.
And to be recognized –
could become what we discern.

Oh, how we laughed:
to have been told;
to have been informed,
of what?

So from what we laughed
we relinquished –
in order for our life.

As If

As if we were seen
straight into,
we could be as if:
we stumbled upon imbalance
and such finding pushed away,
just once more.
And for just once,
we could have become
untethered.
Unspeakable,
we may yet become.

Wavelengths

Leaving when they do,
arriving is all the same.

They could be of shooting stars,
from deep sea currents,
so abrupt and loud;
vibrations in voice,
winds sweeping to be,
screams of play,
washing over of the sun as it passes to the next,
raindrops beating down,
may become lightning bugs in their passage on and off.
Here and elsewhere,
bewitching into
every night.
Drawn we are:
to them we could go.

For once they are here they are gone the next:
it may be no matter
because here again they came; here again they may always
be arriving.

Together

What I see,
what I saw –
to see within again,
can look out again.
Learning to see together,
we keep seeing.

With Ease

Eyes for intent,
laughter of ease,
closeness of shared need –
arms in protection,
they help us to see
where we want to be;
an ineffable feeling, we found –
when we find once more that it is there
we already are.
We found we wanted it still.

Elusive

Could you not love it –
when what has escaped you
is what you too so fled?
Could you love how it feels
to meet face to face
with all you could ever perceive,
might you want again?

Golden

Eyes of gold reflection:
could only light us too –
significant in imagination,
elemental in happening,
profound for us:
as we noted that while once
we looked at silver eyes
as if they could have been
our own,
subsequently we saw absence
of matter in this world –
because that was our way
to ours yet again;
dusted in gold.
We mirrored the reflection to be
all we saw,
as we could have been one in the same yet again.

Our Terms

We thought –
and from such deliverance too
came us;
that from which
we decided on our terms
to be greater than.
Unanimously:
though not by time,
not by tangible exhibit
nor by assessment.
Arisen: from primordial will.
Which in turn,
cared for her so
we cared for us all.

Disarm Us

Oh, how unearthed we were cast –
when but the faintest of motions
from outside us,
became us we interrupted.

We arrived to the beach,
contemplated a boulder for which to sit –
and so looked ahead to the serenity
of hearing the bay waves lull,
alone.
Of watching the birds dance quid pro quo,
alone.
Utterly enamored with these spectroscopic
happenings –
wishing to be inside,
too.

Because vibrance as fragmented,
was all it could have seen
to engender us the same.
Though that alone –
was a concept void; nonexistent.
For to have not:
moved our pen the way we wanted!
Heard the bay waves the way we wanted!
Seen the birds dance the way we wanted!
Found us aflame,
to do just that; to be more than that.

Knocked from the course only
because only one became another –
to spiral from its' own.

After that they all came,
amidst each other.
Splintered was our interpretation;
our confusion followed
of that beautiful beach.

To be found the opposite of enchanting: all feelings undone.

To go from there may be up –
could only *up* be more formidable
than there.

So to a new land we went; a new beach we were found;
one so beautiful in that we chose it,
for which we created.

The people on the beach called for us.

To hear them hurt;
for our rocks from which we sat
were of design incomparable.
For such reason the same,
to hear them we were loved.

Though could their ears
never see us –
we held responsibility
to foster more.

By elementary envisioning once more;
by progression,
we emanated a beauty
made to shatter the sky
and crumble these walls –
we again saw all,
and then past.
Inevitably,
the once disarming worries of others
became silence,
and in place:
our desires for what else; what more.

Ultimately and so soon we found
that we had arrived,
at the beach one last time –
suddenly all the boulders would have supported us fine,
suddenly yet we joined with one.
As we saw it support more than enough,
we gasped in a grin at its display
that we required more than
enough.

The sun's rays healed our faces:
flooding through us,
draining.

For there,
in a moment's time we had looked past:
only into.

Enthralled with purple tones,
we moved our pen –
the furthest removed from reservation.
Bay waves invited us in,
dancing birds swooped down to extend our hand.
As lifted as we were,
still we saw.

Never alone,
could only have thought it so.
Having evaded the push,
we pulled once more
as we had thought of everything –
and so had everything.

If we wanted to see, then we did.
And if we wanted something else, then we did that too.

The Regression Forth

Oh, how to have felt:
through opening,
reminding,
that after all,
we were embraced
in place,
rather than drowned in a second thought.

After that, they lost all thought;
themselves.
For they had given way,
as always.

The Lowered Eye

Felt what it may,
witnessing ourselves, collected –
leveled to *be* them all; it all:
an entity further marginalized –
though only seemingly so
to the lowered eye.
For it could never be told,
as the exhibition left
before ever to be thought of again –
a ceaseless speculation,
a ceaseless circulation of feeling ever-changing,
demanded the urgent question:
May we too, pick up and move things around?
May we heighten our gaze?

Where We Were

The frozen lull,
above choosing to sleep:
of falling asleep,
near.
Laying on a beach,
strangers ever present
though not always for there.
With the cognition
in ways both met and obscure,
that we may be at peace;
at ease with reality.
Indeed, the world has –
for an unmistakable moment in time
and for a moment free of time,
appeared to have met you where you were.

Undertow

We lit up everywhere:
electrified,
time with time again –
best we give what it gave
and allow flight forward.
Opposed to none other,
and none other could ponder such reason.
Reason could not be pondered,
for what pulled us forward
may be reason enough for before,
and may be reason that for which forward be unlocked for all.

Uproar

With us all that day they lingered;
as instantaneously we wondered
in having seen them together,
could it be more if we act *for*,
rather not *from* what we freed from thought.
Immensely so,
if we may be wishing
for them ablaze.

Transcendence

All from which we were found,
we effected further through time:
so as to forth be freed;
so as to forever break these chains.

www.ingramcontent.com/pod-product-compliance
Lightning Source LLC
Chambersburg PA
CBHW070633150426
42811CB00050B/289